The Heart of a Christian Leader

Eric Ferguson

The Heart of a Christian Leader

By Eric Ferguson

Metanoia Missions International

ISBN 978-0-9835821-2-0

Printed in the United States of America

© Metanoia Missions International 2012

All rights reserved.

No portion of this book may be reproduced
in any form without the written permission of the author.

Scripture quotations taken from
THE HOLY BIBLE, NEW INTERNATIONAL VERSION®, NIV®
Copyright © 1973, 1978, 1984, 2011 by Biblica, Inc.™
Used by permission. All rights reserved worldwide."

Cover art by Shahzad Kashif/grapesart

Book design by Lorinda Gray/Ragamuffin Creative

www.ragamuffincreative.com

The Heart of a Christian Leader

Eric Ferguson

CONTENTS

Foreword 6

Introduction 9

1. A Heart Identified in Christ 15

2. A Pure Heart 23

3. A Heart Open to Correction 33

4. Study Questions 41

5. Answer Key 47

The Heart of a Christian Leader

FOREWORD

Not many months before my father went to be with the Lord, he told me something I've cherished ever since. He said that from time to time he would receive phone calls from young men who were training for the ministry. Knowing my father was then in his late eighties, they would ask him if they could come by so he could pray over them. They all had one thing in common; they wanted his mantle. With a twinkle in his eye my father told me, "David, they all want my mantle, but no one wants my sack cloth and ashes."

True leadership is never mass produced in some famous Bible College or School of Divinity. You don't acquire it by listening to lectures, studying books, listening to tapes, or attending conferences or seminars. While many of these things may prove beneficial they fall short of one vital imperative, and that is, time alone with Jesus.

Following a night spent in prayer, Jesus came down from the mountain and appointed twelve men who later became known as the twelve apostles. Mark informs us that "…He appointed twelve that they might be with Him, and that He might send them out to preach…" Notice, if you will, the order here. First they were to spend time with Him. Only then were they to go out to preach. Godly and effective leadership begins by spending time with Jesus. "Take my yoke upon you and learn of Me…"

The principles that my friend Eric shares in this small but powerful book were learned by attending the College of Experience. They are vital and essential truths for anyone sensing a call to the ministry.

Read them on your knees and allow the Spirit of God to weave them into the very fabric of your life. You will be glad someday that you did!

David Ravenhill

INTRODUCTION

As one studies the various aspects of leadership, it should become quite evident that there is a difference between a Christian leader and a non-Christian or secular leader. According to leadership experts, the definition of leadership is simply *influence*. That is, being a leader is having an influence on someone. I actually like to consider leadership the art of having followers. In other words, you are a true leader if and only if people are following you. So if a person has followers, then he or she will of course have some sort of influence on his or her followers.

Researchers tell us that the average person will influence close to ten thousand people in his or her lifetime. Can you imagine that? Each and every one of us has the opportunity to influence ten thousand people during our lifetime. The thought that you and I have the potential to impact over ten thousand

The Heart of a Christian Leader

individuals is absolutely overwhelming. However, what is even more overwhelming is the fact that this statistic of having an influence on ten thousand people isn't just limited to Christian leaders. It includes Christians and non-Christians alike!

This closing statement brings me back to what I first mentioned: there is a difference between a Christian and non-Christian leader. You see, the difference between a Christian and a non-Christian leader is the direction in which he or she is leading people. The apostle Paul tells us in Ephesians 5:1 "Be imitators of God, therefore, as dearly beloved children," and in 1 Corinthians 4:6 he says, "Therefore I urge you to imitate me." The apostle really makes it clear what direction the Christian leader should be headed in when he said, "Follow my example as I follow the example of Christ" (1 Cor. 11:1).

As Christian leaders, our motive should be to lead people toward or closer to Christ. A Christian leader's desire should be to set an example for others to follow. Secular leaders, on the other hand, tend to be more focused on power, position, money, and fame. Therefore, the difference between true *Christian leadership* and just plain *leadership* is the motive of the heart.

There are many characteristics of a Christian leader's heart; however, I would only like to discuss three of them. From Corinth, Paul wrote a letter to the people in Rome to prepare them for his upcoming visit. In this writing to the Romans, Paul discusses many facets of the Christian faith and goes into great detail, explaining what justification by faith and the righteousness of God are.

I'm sure Paul had every intention of going to Rome, sitting down with the church leaders, and discussing these topics in more detail. However, as we know, Paul never made it to Rome like he thought he would. Instead, he only made it there as a prisoner. It was in Rome where Paul and Peter were both martyred for their dedication to Jesus Christ. I find this quite interesting. Here was this man Paul, who was previously named Saul, writing a very deep, theologically sound letter to the church of Rome. In fact, it is from this particular letter that the body of Christ has taken much of its doctrine. Yet isn't it interesting that only a few years prior to this letter, Paul, or at the time Saul, was persecuting and killing Christians for their belief in Christ.

In Acts 7, when Stephen, the mighty man of God, was giving his speech before the Sanhedrin, it was Saul who stood by and gave his approval to stone Stephen. However, in just a few short years we find Paul writing powerful, Holy Spirit–filled letters to the believers in various parts of the world. So what

The Heart of a Christian Leader

happened? Paul tells us exactly what happened to him in Romans 15:15–16: "I have written you quite boldly on some points, as if to remind you of them again, *because of the Grace God gave me* to be a minister of Christ Jesus to the Gentiles with the priestly duty of proclaiming the Gospel of God."

Paul was a well-educated man. He was an incredible scholar who sat under some of the very best teachers, so he could have defended himself by using his excellent education and training. He could have explained that he had a life-changing encounter with God in the middle of the street, but he didn't. He simply said that because of the grace God had given him, he was able to write what he was writing. From this statement, it is very clear that Paul was completely identified in Christ. When God calls someone into a place of influence, or in other words, a place of leadership, it is not because the person has earned it or even deserves it. It was made possible because of God's grace and mercy and His divine favor.

According to *Nelson's Illustrated Bible Dictionary*, the word grace means "Favor or kindness shown without regard to the worth or merit of the one who receives it and in spite of what that same person deserves."[1] We are who we are because of God's unmerited favor, or in other words, by His grace.

---

[1] Herbert Lockyer, ed., Nelson's Illustrated Bible Dictionary. (Nashville, TN: Thomas Nelson, 1986), 443.

CHAPTER 1

A Heart Identified in Christ

We as Christians are who we are because of the grace of Jesus Christ. Consider Paul once again. He didn't receive his identity from his ability to lead. He didn't receive his identity from his education. He didn't receive his identity from the experience he had with God on the road to Damascus. Paul's identity came from who he was in Jesus Christ. His heart was identified in Jesus Christ. Paul was who he was by the grace of God.

It should be the same way with us as Christian leaders. Our identity should not come from who we are as leaders; our identity should come from who we are in Christ. When our churches are doing well and we have large crowds of people, we must understand that it's not because of us, it's because God is moving through us. When our ministries are growing and

The Heart of a Christian Leader

getting people's attention, it's not because we are God's gift to the world or on the cutting edge. They are growing because of God's grace.

We cannot fall into the trap of thinking that our churches or ministries are all about us and our ability to lead, because when we do, we set ourselves up for failure. Everything we do must be based on our identity in Christ. We cannot lead just to get egos stroked by other people. We cannot be in leadership just to feel good about ourselves and our accomplishments.

We cannot lead based on our egos, because what happens to us when we are doing everything we possibly can but things just aren't going well? What happens when we've been through all the classes, we've studied all the books, we've done everything we know we should do, but we just aren't experiencing the growth and success we think we should have? Do we get down and discouraged like we have seen so many other Christian leaders do? Do we get upset and frustrated to the point where it begins to affect those around us? Do we begin to compare ourselves to other leaders and question our own abilities or calling? We do when we are leading from our own strength, ability, and knowledge instead of relying on God. Without strong foundations of God's grace in our lives and hearts that are identified with Christ, everything we do as leaders will be tainted with a touch of humanism. However, when we lead from our identity in Christ, we realize that there is so much more than ourselves, numbers, recognition, and fame.

In 1998 I started a college and career ministry in Louisville, Kentucky. Before I arrived in Louisville, there were a lot of problems, and the rumor was that the college and career pastor actually left the church and used the people in the college and career ministry to pioneer a church on the other side of town. However, even with this present instability and the senior pastor's skepticism of a college and career ministry, I really felt I could turn things around and grow a thriving, dynamic ministry. I remember thinking to myself, *I have the education, I have the experience as a leader, and I have a lot of great ideas.* I believed that I could really make things happen. But the problem was that I was concentrating on what I could do and failed to recognize that maybe God had other plans or another way that He desired things to be done.

I remember doing everything possible to grow a ministry. I called everyone. I sent out postcards. I emailed everyone. I would take some of my leaders with me for home and hospital visitations. I would take people out to eat. My wife and I were constantly having people over for dinner. Anything and everything a person could do, I did it. However, the ministry wasn't growing like I wanted it to, so I started to get frustrated and discouraged.

After several more months of frustration and feeling like a failure, the Lord finally spoke to me and revealed something to me: My identity was in the success of the ministry! My identity was in my ability to grow a ministry and not in Jesus Christ! At that moment, I realized that I needed to change my focus and that I needed to be re-identified in Christ. By doing so, it took my focus off of what I could do and put my focus back on Christ. It truly was a defining moment for me.

I wish I could say that from that moment on our ministry there in Louisville, Kentucky, really took off and grew by leaps and bounds, but it didn't. Sure, it kept growing, and we kept seeing lives changed, but not to the extent I had originally hoped for. However, I am proud to say that pastors, missionaries, teachers, worship leaders, Christian business owners, and a variety of church lay leaders were birthed out of the ministry God entrusted to us there in Kentucky. Scottish minister George Morrison stated it well when he said, "Do not waste too much time measuring ourselves…leave your usefulness to God to estimate."

In the passage in Romans that we are addressing, Paul told the Romans that he wasn't leading because of some great track record or ministry success; rather he was leading by the grace of God. You see, when we are afraid to step out in faith, we must cling to our identity in Christ. When we are unsure and insecure in ourselves, we need to find our security in Jesus Christ. This should be our goal. Christian leaders need to get to the point where they say that they are leading only by the grace of God. We don't always have to figure everything out, like is often the tendency of a leader; we just need to rely on God and the grace He offers us.

Warren Wiersbe once said, "What life does to us depends on what life finds in us, and that is where the grace of God comes in." Christian leaders must comprehend that we are what we are by the grace of God. If we are leading something or doing something because it gives us a boost to our self-esteem and makes us feel good, we should stop doing it. Remember, our goal as Christian leaders is to lead people to Christ or help them along in their walk with Him, not to get people just to follow us.

Here is a good question that each one of us needs to ask ourselves: "What do we do when we begin to lead?" The answer can be found in Romans 15:16: "To be a minister of Christ Jesus to the Gentiles *with the priestly* duty of proclaiming the Gospel of God, so that the Gentiles might become an offering acceptable to God, sanctified by the Holy Spirit."

We need to stop for a moment and consider what Paul was saying here. He said that he was a minister of Jesus Christ with priestly duties. This terminology that he uses—priestly duties—comes from the Old Testament responsibilities of the priests in the temple. In the Old Testament, the priests would make sacrifices unto God on behalf of the people. In other words, the priest would stand in the gap between God and the people. When Paul stood in the gap between God and the Gentiles, he would preach the gospel. He was saying that just like the priest in the Old Testament would stand in the gap between God and the people, he too was standing in the gap between God and the Gentiles. He was doing everything he could, out of his identity in Christ, to bring people closer to God. Our job as Christian leaders is to lead people to Jesus Christ. This is impossible to do if our hearts are not fully identified in Jesus Christ. If our hearts are not identified in Jesus Christ, then we might be leading people, but where are we leading them?

Ponder on these two questions:
1) Where do I get my identity?
2) Where am I leading people?

CHAPTER 2

A Pure Heart

A Christian leader's heart must be and remain pure. I specifically stated that the Christian leader's heart must be and remain pure because when we start in leadership, the majority of us start with a pure heart and pure motives. We usually get involved in the leadership of the church because we truly have a passion and desire to help people, and we want to be a part of building the kingdom of God. However, what often happens with time is the Christian leader goes through the fire, so to speak, and his heart begins to change.

Pastor Andy Stanley said, "Life can be hard on the heart. The world is full of outside influences that have the power to disrupt the rhythm of your heart. Over time you develop habits that slowly erode your heart's

The Heart of a Christian Leader

sensitivity."[2] Maybe he was let down one too many times and now his heart is starting to be affected. Or maybe he had great success in ministry and it has begun to affect his heart and motives. For these very reasons, it is vitally important to guard our hearts and focus on our identity in Christ.

I know of a youth pastor who was planning a huge youth conference for the youth of his region. He had everything planned, —the speakers, the lodging, the transportation; he even had the event advertised in several Christian magazines. He was setting himself up for a successful conference and still had time to cover any last- minute details. However, with the conference just a few months away, his senior pastor came to him and told him that he felt he was supposed to have a conference on that same weekend, so he told the youth pastor to post-pone his event.

But something happened; the youth pastor didn't guard his heart and allowed his heart to become bitter. When he went back to his youth group of over four hundred, he told them that the senior pastor was making them cancel their youth conference so that he could host his own conference instead.

Because of the way this youth pastor presented the news, just about all of the youth were hurt and

---

[2] Andy Stanley, *It Came from Within!: The Shocking truth of What Lurks in the Heart.*, Andy Stanley, (Sisters, OR Oregon: Multnomah, 2006), 20.

upset, and their hearts began to turn against the senior pastor. Instead of presenting the youth with the pastor's vision and the great idea of having a church-wide conference, the youth pastor allowed his own hurt and disappointment to affect his heart. A year or so later, when this youth pastor resigned from the church and moved out of town, the majority of the youth stopped attending the church as well. In fact, several years later, the church still struggled with establishing a powerful, fruitful youth ministry. It is vitally important to always remember that our hearts will determine where we are leading the people!

The Apostle Paul wrote to his spiritual son Timothy,:

> "Nevertheless, the firm foundation of God stands, having this seal, "'The Lord knows those who are His,'" and, "'Let everyone who names the name of the Lord abstain from wickedness.'" Now in a large house there are not only vessels of wood and of earthenware, and some to honor and some to dishonor. Therefore, as a man cleanses himself from these things, he will be a vessel of honor, sanctified, useful to the Master, prepared for every good work." (2 Timothy. 2:19-22 NIV).

According to this passage of Scripture, we have a choice as to about what kind of vessel we will be. We can either be vessels of honor or vessels of dishonor. God is looking for vessels of honor. God is looking for Christian leaders who have hearts that are pure and uncontaminated. As Paul says, "God is looking for vessels of honor, sanctified, and useful to the Master, prepared for every good work." When we, as Christian leaders, make the decision to keep our hearts pure and live according to God's Word, Paul says that we will become vessels of honor, sanctified, and useful to the Master, Jesus Christ. I love the fact that Paul uses the word sanctified, because this paints such a vivid picture.

The word sanctified means set apart.[3] Paul is saying that if we choose to keep a pure heart, we will then be sanctified unto the Lord and we will then be prepared for every good work.

Consider this illustration. Here in Nicaragua, the police have a very strong presence. When I take my children to school in the morning, there are random check points. When we travel out to the orphanage, we pass by other check points. When we travel up to the coffee farms in the northern part of the country, we are almost always stopped for random reasons. It

---

[3] Ethelbert W. Bullinger, A Critical Lexicon and Concordance to the English and Greek New Testament. (Grand Rapids, MI: Zondervan, 1975), 660.

is not uncommon to be pulled over throughout the course of a normal day just so the police can check your license and registration.

The police here, like in other countries, have been delegated a particular amount of authority and seem to use it to the maximum. The police here have various commissioners who serve as the big bosses over various departments of the police force. We have had several of these commissioners as members of our church, so I can tell you from personal observation that they have a lot of authority and have the respect of their fellow police officers.

A nice perk that comes with being a police commissioner here in Nicaragua is that fact that you are designated an SUV and an official police chauffeur. In fact, depending on the office you hold as a commissioner, it is not uncommon to see a commissioner being escorted by other armed officers as well as his assigned chauffeur. No matter where these commissioners are in Nicaragua, no matter what time of day it is or what is going on, these high-ranking commissioners have access to their SUV and its driver. Now if for some reason a lower-ranking officer came along and tried to use this high-ranking commissioner's SUV and driver, he would be in big trouble because this SUV has been sanctified for the police commissioner. This SUV and driver have been

The Heart of a Christian Leader

set apart for one purpose and one purpose only—to serve this high-ranking commissioner.

When our hearts are pure before the Lord, we too are set-apart for a high-ranking officer. In fact, He is the highest-ranking officer ever; He is the King of Kings and the Lord of Lords. The Christian leader who has a pure heart has been set apart (sanctified) for the Lord. Because this leader has been set apart, he is a powerful tool in the hand of God and will make an incredible impact on the world around him.

David was one of those people who had a pure heart and was sanctified for the work of the Lord. When the prophet Samuel came to Jesse to anoint one of his sons to become the future king, Samuel chose the least likely of the eight boys. Over all the sons of Jesse, Samuel chose a teenage boy named David. The reason why the prophet Samuel chose David was because of his heart. "But the Lord said to Samuel, referring to Eliab, one of David's older brothers, 'Do not consider his appearance or his height, for I have rejected him. The Lord does not look at the things that man looks at. Man looks at the outward appearance, but the Lord looks at the heart'" (1 Sam. 16:7).

The Lord chose this little shepherd boy to be the future king because he had a pure heart. It wasn't because he was the most talented. It wasn't because he was a natural-born leader. It wasn't because he had a great education or a lot of leadership experience. God chose him because he had a pure heart. In fact, the Bible even says in 1 Samuel 13:14, when referring to David taking the place of Saul as king, *"The Lord has sought out a man after His own heart."* Because of David's pure heart, he was used mightily by the Lord.

It is interesting that even though David's heart was pure, and even though God chose David and anointed him as king, David still fell into sin. Sure, David led nations and armies for the Lord, yet there was a time when his heart wasn't pure and he fell into adultery with Bathsheba. This man who had so much going for him—this man who was so hungry for the things of God and who was literally selected to be king because of his pure heart—fell and fell hard.

Let's face it: there are times when we as Christian leaders are going to really mess up. There are times when we might even fall flat on our faces, just like David did. David's heart slowly drifted away from God, and he began to lose his identity in God. Praise God, though, because David listened to the prophet Nathan and got his act back together. In fact, in Psalm 51 we can see how David humbled himself and made his heart right before God once again. David cries out in verses 1 and 2, "Have mercy on me, O God,

The Heart of a Christian Leader

according to your unfailing love; according to your great compassion blot out my transgressions. Wash away all my iniquity and cleanse me from my sin." Then in verse 10 he says, "Create in me a pure heart, O God, and renew a steadfast spirit within me." David truly was a man of God, who, if truth be told, wanted to do what was right. Because he humbled himself before the Lord, God continued to use him for His glory and honor.

As Christian leaders, we must recognize that we are all vulnerable and have natural-born tendencies to be drawn away from God. For this reason, we must continually check the condition of our hearts. It is also extremely important for us as Christian leaders to constantly apply 1 John 1:9 to our lives: "If you confess your sins, he is faithful and just to forgive us our sins and purify us from all unrighteousness." If we've messed up, we must ask for forgiveness. If we have issues or strongholds in our lives, we must confess them, ask for help, and allow the Holy Spirit to come in and work on our hearts. We cannot afford to be afraid of what people might think, and we cannot be afraid of being embarrassed. We need to do what it takes to get our hearts right before God. The most important thing is the condition of each and every one of our hearts before the Lord.

Ponder on these two questions:
1) Are you a vessel of honor, sanctified unto the Lord?
2) Is your heart as pure today as it was the day you began to serve as a leader?

CHAPTER 3

A Heart Open to Correction

The heart of the Christian leader should always be open to correction. Unfortunately many leaders think that once they have arrived at a particular level of leadership or achieved a particular position of authority, they no longer have to be open to or listen to people who are offering them correction. However, this is a lie straight from the enemy. If a person has hardened his or her heart and is not open to receive correction, that means pride has set in, and as we all know, pride is the root of all sin. Well-known speaker and author Dr. Henry T. Blackaby suggests that leaders need to be proactive and seek at least two people as accountability partners and give them the freedom to question you and correct you when needed.

The Heart of a Christian Leader

A friend of mine, David Ravenhill, recently forwarded me an exceptionally impressive protocol and set of standards from a very well-known and well-respected prophet. Even though this man is recognized for his gift and is an authoritative voice among Charismatic Christian leaders, he still appears to be wise and humble enough to recognize his need for accountability and when necessary, possible correction. This man of God wrote the following for the protocol and standards of his ministry:

> I commit to continuing in accountability to a safe and loving authority whom I believe will support me and help me walk in integrity. I will not remove myself from this process even if painful to me and/or it seems that those to whom I am accountable are not treating me fairly.

What an incredible declaration this man of God is making. Even if he is uncomfortable or believes his spiritual authorities are being unjust, he will remain submissive to their authority and will remain accountable to them. The truth is that it is very difficult today to find people in leadership with hearts like this. Most people would rather reject the notion of being corrected and continue with their present way of doing things. Unfortunately, very few leaders are willing to, as they say, swallow their pride and maintain a teachable heart.

Let's look at what the Word of God has to say about pride.

> To fear the Lord is to hate evil; I hate pride and arrogance, evil behavior and perverse speech. (Prov. 8:13)

> When pride comes, then comes disgrace, but with humility comes wisdom. (Prov. 11:2)

> Pride goes before destruction, a haughty spirit before a fall. (Prov. 16:18)

Once we have hardened our hearts and closed ourselves off to correction, we have allowed pride to set in. Once pride has set in, it is just a matter of time until we fall. Solomon stated very clearly in Proverbs that if we have proud hearts, then we are headed for destruction. Once again, using the life of David as an illustration, we can see how David was open to receive correction. In 2 Samuel 12, the prophet Nathan came to King David and rebuked him. The prophet used a story to illustrate how awful David had been acting and how he was not living right. At

The Heart of a Christian Leader

this point, David had a very important decision to make. He could have used his power and position as king to have the prophet removed from his presence or even killed and continued on with his life of sin, or he could have taken to heart what the prophet Nathan shared with him and made things right. Thankfully for David's soul's sake, he had an open heart and received correction from Nathan.

I think it is important to point out here that just because David repented and made things right with God didn't mean there were not circumstances that came along with his sin. Remember the law of motion? For every action, there is an equal or greater reaction. Second Samuel 12 says that because of David's sin, the sword would never leave his house; that out of his own household calamity would come upon him; that his very wife would have sexual relations in broad daylight where all Israel would see; and that the son born as a result of his adulterous affair with Bathsheba would die.

That is one of the things about being a leader: our actions, decisions, and behaviors have a greater effect on more people. Why? Because we are leaders, we have an influence on others. For this reason, we need to be identified in Christ all the days of our lives, we need to keep our hearts pure before the Lord, and we need to continually remain open to correction.

Remember, as a Christian leader, your actions aren't just affecting you but are affecting everyone around you and all of those you have an influence on.

I would like to close with a few of Solomon's sayings.

> The corrections of discipline are the way to life. (Prov. 6:23b)

> He who hates correction will die!
> (Prov. 15:10b)

> He who hates correction is stupid.
> (Prov. 12:1b)

> He who heeds discipline shows the way to life, but whoever ignores correction leads others astray. (Prov. 10:17)

This last one should really hit home for us as Christian leaders. Whoever ignores correction *leads* others astray. If we ignore correction, we are leading others astray. An interesting point to remember here is that we aren't just talking about the people you are leading right now or those who are involved with you in some aspect of ministry. Solomon is referring to the ten thousand potential people you will influence at some point in your life.

The Heart of a Christian Leader

Wow! Now that should be a reality check for each and every one of us! Our unwillingness to listen to the correction of others could cause us to potentially lead ten thousand people astray. To really make this point hit home, Matthew 12:36, Luke 16:2, Romans 14:12, Hebrews 4:13, and Romans 3:19 say that we will all be held accountable for what we have done on the day when we stand before God. Now I don't know about you, but I do not want to be held accountable for leading ten thousand people astray. I recognize that my responsibility as a Christian leader is to lead people to Christ, not away from Him. I want to purpose in my heart to remain open to the correction of my brothers and sisters in Christ.

Ponder on these two questions:
1) Is your heart open to correction?
2) On the day when you are called to give an account for your life, how many of those potential ten thousand people will have been led astray by your actions, behaviors, and decisions?

CHAPTER 4

Study Questions
Introduction

1) Experts say that the basic definition of leadership is
_____
_____

2) What is the difference between a Christian leader and a non-Christian leader?
_____
_____

3) Researchers say that the average person will influence _____ people in his/her lifetime.

4) In Ephesians 5:1, Paul says we should be
_____
_____

The Heart of a Christian Leader

5) As Christian leaders, our motive should be to

_____

_____

6) The greatest difference between true Christian leadership and non-Christian or secular leadership is

_____

_____

7) We are who we are by _____

_____

Study Questions
Chapter 1: A Heart Identified in Christ

1. Our identity should come from who we are in

_____

_____

2. In Romans 15:15, Paul said he was leading by

_____

_____

3. Why do our churches and/or ministries grow?

_____

_____

4. True or False: Many of us get our identity in ministry from numbers and success.

5. What should we do if we are doing something out of selfish motives or to boost our self-esteem?

_____

6. What was Paul's priestly duty to the Gentiles?

_____
_____

Study Questions
Chapter 2: A Pure Heart

1. True or False: It is hard to keep one's heart pure.

Explain your answer:

_____
_____
_____
_____
_____
_____
_____

2. What type of vessel should we strive to be?

_____

The Heart of a Christian Leader

3. What type of Christian leader is God looking for?

_____

_____

4. The Lord doesn't look at the outward appearances, but He looks at the _____

5. Why did God choose David? (Read 1 Sam. 13:14.)

_____

6. True or False: If our hearts are pure, we will never be vulnerable to temptation.

Explain your answer:

_____
_____
_____
_____
_____
_____
_____
_____

7. If we have fallen short as leaders, what do we need to do?

_____
_____
_____

Study Questions
Chapter 3: A Heart Open to Correction

1. When should a Christian leader's heart be open to correction?

_____

2. True or False: Dr. Blackaby says we should be proactive and look for accountability partners.

3. According to Proverbs 11:2, what comes after pride? _____.

4. What happens to those who hate correction (Prov. 15:10)? _____

5. As leaders, Proverbs 10:17 tells us that if we ignore correction, we will

_____
_____
_____

6. When summarized, what conclusion do Matthew 12:36, Luke 16:2, and Romans 14:2 draw?

_____
_____
_____

CHAPTER 5:

Answer Key
Introduction

1) Experts say that the basic definition of leadership is **influence**.

2) What is the difference between a Christian leader and a non-Christian leader? **The direction in which they lead people.**

3) Researchers say that the average person will influence **ten thousand** people in his/her lifetime.

4) In Ephesians 5:1, Paul says we should be **imitators of God.**

5) As Christian leaders, our motive should be to **lead people toward or closer to Christ.**

6) The greatest difference between true Christian leadership and non-Christian or secular leadership is **the motive of the heart.**

7) We are who we are by **God's grace.**

The Heart of a Christian Leader

Answer Key
Chapter 1: A Heart Identified in Christ

1. Our identity should come from who we are in **Jesus Christ.**

2. In Romans 15:15, Paul said he was leading by **the grace of God.**

3. Why do our churches and/or ministries grow? **Because of God's grace.**

4. **True** or False: Many of us get our identity in ministry from numbers and success.

5. What should we do if we are doing something out of selfish motives or to boost our self-esteem? **Stop doing it.**

6. What was Paul's priestly duty to the Gentiles? **Proclaiming the gospel of God.**

Answer Key
Chapter 2: A Pure Heart

1. **True** or False: It is hard to keep one's heart pure.

Explain your answer: _____
_____
_____
_____

2. What type of vessel should we strive to be? **Vessel of honor.**

3. What type of Christian leader is God looking for? **Pure and uncontaminated.**

4. The Lord doesn't look at the outward appearances, but He looks at the **heart.**

5. Why did God choose David? **Because of his heart.** (Read 1 Sam. 13:14.)

6. True or **False**. If our hearts are pure, we will never be vulnerable to temptation.

Explain your answer: _____
_____

7. If we have fallen short as leaders, what do we need to do? **Confess our sins and ask for forgiveness.**

The Heart of a Christian Leader

Answer Key
Chapter 3: A Heart Open to Correction

1. When should a Christian leader's heart be open to correction? **Always.**

2. **True** or False: Dr. Blackaby says we should be proactive and look for accountability partners.

3. According to Proverbs 11:2, what comes after pride? **Disgrace.**

4. What happens to those who hate correction (Prov. 15:10)? **They will die.**

5. As leaders, Proverbs 10:17 tells us that if we ignore correction we will **lead others astray.**

6. When summarized, what conclusion do Matthew 12:36, Luke 16:2, and Romans 14:2 draw? **We will all be held accountable to God.**

Other books by Eric Ferguson

We Are Called to This

Discovering Your Way In Marriage

The Leader's Little Quote Book

Eric's Blog Book

El Principio de la Sabiduria